M000029277

LIFE
POKER

Making the best decisions with
the cards you've been dealt

KWANTRELL GREEN

Life Poker

Copyright © 2018 by Kwantrell Green. All rights reserved. This book or any portion thereof may not be reproduced or used in any manner whatsoever without the express written permission of the author except for the use of brief quotations in a book review.

Printed in the United States of America

First Printing, 2018

ISBN: 978-0-9997807-8-7

Publishers:
Above The Line Press
McKinney, TX
www.abovethelinepress.com

DEDICATION

I dedicate this book to my grandmother who played an influential role in my upbringing. I love you dearly, Ms. Myrtis M. Tobias November 4, 1939 to May 1, 2010.

TABLE OF CONTENTS

INTRODUCTION

What is your purpose in life? Why would you want to be the best person that you can possibly be? These are burning questions that most people find themselves consistently trying to figure out. Life itself can be very challenging at times, but if you never take full control of it, you can be dealt a bad hand and lose your self-esteem, self-respect, and self-awareness. The good news is that all of life's adversity can be turned into infinite opportunities if you know how to play your cards right. You don't have to accept the consequences, but yet embrace life's rewards.

With every obstacle faced, a chance to succeed presents itself. You either choose to progress through life or regress. I once read there are three types of people in this world, those who **MAKE** things happen, those who **WATCH** what happens, and there are those who sit around and **WONDER** what happens. This has resonated with me for the past 15 years of my life. I found myself both watching and making things happen but decided to start making things happen 100 percent of the time. From that point on, *Life Poker* was born. This concept was created by observation of others in which I saw mirror images in my own personal situations. I realized that individuals didn't know how to cope with adversity, couldn't see the big picture, or most times wound up settling for less. I then decided to share my thoughts and ideas along with a few personal examples, with the intent of teaching how to win at this game called life.

Life Poker is about you, the difficulties you endure, and the curve balls life throws when things seem to be going well. Life itself is about decision, purpose, and story. Our encounters along with the adversity we endure may very well be messages to uplift your fellow man. The test we experience can certainly be a testimony for others going through similar situations. *Life Poker* serves as a guide to encourage you to identify external factors that may be hindering your growth, but also internal factors to hold yourself accountable. Each chapter depicts a situation that you either may have gone through or are possibly weathering through at the moment. The aim of this book is to help you figure out who you are, your purpose, and who you want to become moving forward. It's time for you to stop being average and start achieving greatness.

I'm here to let you know, ***"Sometimes we can't control the cards that we are dealt in life, but we can control the outcome."***

- Kwantrell D. Green

MOTIVATION

"Motivation is what gets you started, Habit is what keeps you going." – Jim Rohn

You must First Determine the Direction You want to Travel in

Follow Your Dreams

First and foremost, you must simply follow your dreams. What are dreams? Dreams can be a succession of images, thoughts, or emotions passing through the mind during sleep. Dreams can be an aspiration, a goal, or even passion of where you want to be in life. Dreams can also be a false sense of perception and euphoria. Simply put, what good are dreams if you don't take the necessary steps towards pursuing them? John Maxwell says, *"A dream becomes reality as result of your actions, and actions are controlled, to a large extent, by your habits."*

See the Big Picture

As individuals we need to see the big picture. Begin by

evaluating both your short and long-term goals, and always expect and be prepared for the unexpected. Far too often, we don't plan to fail, but more so fail to plan. People have the tendency to stay enclosed inside of a box when it comes to life. If we never think outside of the box, how are we going to live outside of the box?

Don't be Afraid to Take the Road Less Traveled

Majority of the time that road requires hard work. These are where lessons are learned. It is true that rewards are appreciated more when earned. Keep in mind that there are no shortcuts in life, and those who have achieved success have put in the necessary time, effort, blood, sweat, and tears.

Invest in Yourself through Time and Effort

Become a Risk Taker

Quite often we spend majority of our time, effort, and sometimes even our lives helping others grow and live out their dreams/aspirations. However, we don't spend much time or hardly any focusing on our own dreams. Friends and family can be our worst critics and serve up the most criticism about things we want accomplished in life. Bill Cosby once said, *"I don't know the key to success, but the key to failure is trying to please everybody."* Over the years during my teaching career, I've taught many students who wanted to better themselves so when they took the step to enroll into school, they would hear things such as why are you going to school for that? You're much better than what you're majoring in? Or, I wouldn't do that if I were you? Those opinions can be very discouraging and disheartening. The first step towards achieving success, happiness, or the desires of your heart, is simply taking risks. How do you know you'll ever be able to fly if you don't spread your wings?

Change Your Perspective

If you want to achieve a different outlook in life you must change your perspective about things. You must change the way you view situations, people, and opinions. Not only do you have to be able to listen effectively, try to look at and understand the other person's point of view before casting judgment. Do not be ignorant to other cultures, religion, etc., just because you were raised a certain way in life. Begin to understand why people feel the way they do, it can be life changing. Keep in mind, your life doesn't get better by chance, it gets better by Change.

Return on Investment (ROI)

In the business world, a return on investment is basically the money you get back from your invested money. The same is true when you are motivating yourself to improve your surroundings, your job, and your worth. When you invest heavily in yourself, you're creating a better future. A short-term investment in oneself can net a long-term gain of wealth and knowledge. If you were given $1,000 right now, what would you do with it? Most would splurge on things of non-value, some would save, and a few would invest in themselves. Would you buy a brand-new iPhone that's going to create a monthly bill or would you invest in a Roth IRA, a class or certification that will net you a skill to generate additional income?

Focus Your Attention on being Positive

Positive Thoughts

Focus on creating positive thoughts every day and every moment of your life. When situations get rough, you have to be able to find the silver lining in each situation you endure. Everything that happens in our lives is created by the things we say and are also manifested within our thoughts. Be mindful of your thoughts, because your thoughts will most certainly determine your outcome on life.

Positive Attitude

Do you want to be around people with negative attitudes? I shouldn't have to ask that question, but if so, the answer should always be absolutely not. Realize that the pessimist sees difficulty in every opportunity. The optimist sees the opportunity in every difficulty. Attitude is everything; it determines your character and how people perceive you to be.

Positive Environment

You can create your own positive environment. You can choose to be around positive influencers rather than those with negative perceptions. Learning how to manage difficult people around you can be very challenging. You can be surrounded by perfectionist, control freaks, aggressive, defensive, submissive, and creative individuals. Before, we point the finger determine what type of attitude you bring to the environment. You may feel like others can be difficult at times, but the difficult one just maybe you. Self-evaluate and once you determine who you are and what value you bring to the table, you'll set the precedence for an effective environment.

Chapter Assignment

- Challenge yourself with something you know you could never do, and you'll find that you can overcome anything.
- Identify 1-3 things that will add value to your life that you can invest in.
- Identify or create a positive affirmation to motivate yourself each day.
- Identify the type of environment you create, and then decide which one you want to surround yourself in.

HARD WORK/DEDICATION

"All roads that lead to SUCCESS has to pass through Hard Work Boulevard at some point"

You can't be Afraid to Roll Your Sleeves up and go to Work.

Get those Hands Dirty

Life can be very challenging at times, but those that are successful, persevere in spite of difficulties. No one shares your vision or same passion as you do, so therefore you have to lead by example. In my first business as a healthcare agency, I served in the capacity of CEO, server, therapist, bus driver, homemaker, etc. To get where you want to be in life, sometimes you do things you don't want to do in order to get to where you want to be. When things get rough, remind yourself that you're just passing through.

Focus on Progress

Re-direct the energy you put into making excuses into forwarding your progress. *"If you really want to do something, you'll find a way. If you don't, you'll find an excuse."* – Jim Rohn. You're going to hear me say this several times in the future; excuses are monuments of nothingness that builds bridges that lead to nowhere. Those who use these tools of incompetence are masters of nothingness. If you're not working, you're not growing. Don't look at how far you've fallen, but how far you've come.

Pay attention to detail, it matters.

Be Persistent

Keep knocking on those doors because sooner or later one will open for you. People give up easily when there's red tape or if they receive a few no's. That's to be expected when you're trying to accomplish specific tasks. Examine a fisherman, he may go out one day and catch nothing, but return the next and catch an abundance of fish. On your job or in a relationship, you may cast your net 99 times and get nothing but the 100th time may be the right opportunity for you.

Master Your Craft

You can have all the necessary tools in your toolbox, but if you're not using or sharpening them, you are most certainly going to remain stagnant. The best athletes in the world work to master their craft every single day. If you want to beat the best at their game, you have must practice just as hard as the best, to become the best.

Discipline your actions.

Stop Blaming Others

If you make a mistake, own it. Sometimes we just have to look ourselves in the mirror, bite the bullet, and accept responsibility.

Don't Succumb to Temptation

They are all around us and can easily cloud your mind and affect your better judgment. It's easy to get off track and sometimes even more difficult to get back on track, so limit any distractions as often as possible.

Practice good time management

Set aside time each day to focus on specific tasks, but more importantly take time out for you. This book is all about you and your personal growth so take the time out to focus on what's important and apply to your life.

Chapter Assignment

- Define what hard work means to you in your life.
- Identify current distractions in both your personal and professional life.
- Think of a way(s) that you eliminate those distractions and start building healthy habits.

FEAR

"You see things, and say WHY? But I dream things that never were, and say WHY NOT?" – Bernard Shaw

Deal with Problems.

Facing Your Fears

Stare fear directly in the face and declare, "I Refuse to Sink." Self-pity, self-consciousness, and self-conceit will no longer rent space inside of my head.

Dealing with Adversity Can Reveal Progress

Adversity comes in many forms and always presents itself as obstacles. How we deal with adversity only builds character and boosts our confidence to overcome challenges. It reveals qualities inside of us that have been dormant for years and is ready to be awakened.

Put a Hand Up, rather than Look for a Handout.

Identify What You Want and Should Be Doing

Keep in mind that God wants you to have everything your heart desires. Speak things into existence, believe

21

it, and receive it. It may not materialize right away but the signs are all around to reassure that it's coming. Often times we tend not to pay attention to signs or easily get discouraged and stop believing. Your thoughts need to be consistent with what you asked for.

A.C.T. on the Things You Desire

The things you want most in life require Aspiration, Courage, and Timing. Aspire to have, courage to pursue, and seize the moment when it presents itself.

Believe in Yourself and Stop People Pleasing.

Stop Accepting Other's Opinions

If you don't design your own life plan, chances are you'll fall into someone else's plan. And guess what they have planned for you? Not Much! Opinions are just what they are, an opinion. People tend to want to support with facts, but if it doesn't bring value to your life, it doesn't matter.

Stop Living in Fear

Why live in shame? We all make mistakes. Why live in denial? You're only hindering your growth process. Why live in others' shadows? If they don't want more out of life, chances are you won't either.

You are Unique in Your Own Way

Since conception, you were born with unique qualities that differentiate you from everyone else. Once you're able to identify those traits, it's how you use those unique talents that will help shape and control your destiny.

Chapter Assignment

I encourage you to sign-up for my online group and podcast so that we can be able communicate weekly about questions you may have to begin growing and achieving greatness. Let's stomp out fear and go be great together.

LOW SELF-ESTEEM

"Keep away from people who try to belittle your ambitions. Small people always do that, but the really great make you feel that you, too can become great."
— Mark Twain

Living Life below Our Potential

Chronic Low Expectations

You need to view yourself as being great on a consistent frequency. So how do you overcome this chronic problem? I tell my children all the time, I can't want the best for you when you want average for yourself. Signs that you may be underachieving may include taking short cuts in life, making excuses as to why you failed to complete a task, or even expecting others to side with you when you're completely wrong. You can overcome this by simply challenging yourself daily. Start simple to build habits, and then gradually increase those expectations.

Living an Average Lifestyle

You are the Average of the 5 People You Spend the Most Time With

Think about that for a moment. A lot of times the people around you tend to bring you down simply by the way they think. They'll convince you to feel sorry for them and before you know it, you begin feeling sorry for yourself. Out of the group of family/friends you associate with, you may be the one who is ambitious and has aspirations for success but find yourself falling down to a level of complacency where others may be comfortable. Surround yourself with others of like attainment or begin to motivate others to better themselves.

Continue to A.C.T

As mentioned in the previous chapter, things we want most in life requires us to ACT. Aspire to have, courage to pursue, and seize the moment when it presents itself. Deal with any esteem issues that you're aware of before they become foregone problems.

You Determine Your Future.

Japanese Proverb

"Fall seven times, stand up eight."

Master Mental Discipline

We can easily say that we were born to win but conditioned to lose. The teachings and upbringing within certain cultures have modified the way we view things and people. We may have been taught to believe certain things, but when challenged with the truth and/or supporting facts, you'll buck and kick against to defend your beliefs. Don't be afraid to be open-minded, but yet stay true to who you are as an individual.

Chapter Assignment

Take a step back and observe those around you, I want you to practice to listening to what's not being said.

CHANGE…EMBRACE, ACCEPT, ADAPT

"You will never change your life until you change
something you do daily."   – John Maxwell

Self SWOT Analysis

*Identify Strengths, Weakness, Opportunities,
and Threats*

In the business world, this is a strategy used to help
owners make important business decisions.

Yet in life, we can apply this philosophy to help
ourselves become better personally and professionally.
Be ambitious in pursuing your dreams of
entrepreneurship, or may be you want a better job;
whatever it may be, self-evaluate and plan to move
forward.

LIFE POKER SWOT ANALYSIS

STRENGTHS (+)	WEAKNESSES (-)
• Make a list of your best qualities (i.e. personality, attitude, hard worker, etc.) • What unique qualitties you possess that adds value to yourself and others?	• What improvements need to be made? • What personal attributes do you lack as an individual? • How are these negative attributes being perceived by others?

OPPORTUNITIES (+)	THREATS (-)
• List doors that are currently open to you. • List opportunities you can capitalize on. • Identify how your strenghts can create new connections.	• Identify negative things in your life (i.e. people, environment) • How have these things hindered your growth in the past?

Embrace, Accept, & Adapt.

The World is Constantly Changing All Around Us Every Day.

"Opportunity often comes disguised in the form of misfortune or temporary defeat" (Napoleon Hill). Sometimes a situation can be just what it is, but once you're able to adapt. Take control of it, move forward, and don't look back.

Chapter Assignment

Start creating daily positive affirmations. Affirmations are proven methods of self-improvement because they help rewire our brains.

LEADERSHIP

"A leader is one who knows the way, goes the way, and shows the way."   – John Maxwell

Cultivate the Seeds You Plant in People and Most Importantly Your Own Life

Begin by Maintaining that Great Attitude

Being a leader focus on empowering individuals to be great while adding value that inspires GROWTH. With that, being motivated to inspire others growth can impact your leadership skills. Also, having a great attitude will set the tone for anything you do. As a leader you should always be leading by example.

Build a foundation with the 3 – C's

Confidence

If you don't believe in yourself, who else will?

Commitment

Learn how to sacrifice for the things you want most in life.

Character

Requires COURAGE to make tough decisions, SELF-DISCIPLINE to deny your wants and pursue your needs, and finally you should possess INTEGRITY to do right by people and they will do right by you. People will respect you more if you remain honest with them.

Develop Leadership Qualities

- o Be Courageous
- o Challenge Conventional thinking
- o Turn details into action
- o Build hope & Confidence
- o Never Surrender

Chapter Assignment

Write down ways that you will begin to lead your family, friends, and even others on the job. In order to be effective, you have to start the process.

PERCEPTION

"The trouble with most of us is that we would rather be ruined by praise than saved by criticism."
– Norman Vincent Peale

Let's First Begin to Understand Who Exactly You Are

I'm a firm believer in when someone asks my opinion, my exact response is "Do you want me to tell you the truth or do you want me to tell you what you want to hear? Of course, I'm going to give you the truth because we should be GROWING as individuals.

Change the Way You Do Things

Try a new approach especially if the old ways have failed you time and time again. Always think positive and I can't say this enough, CHANGE YOUR HABITS to mimic positivity and productivity, i.e. Every year you make a ham and every year you cut the ends off the ham and every year someone asks you, "Why do you cut the ends off your ham?" (OLD WAY) and every year you reply, "I don't know my mom always did it so I do it too." (COMPLACEMENT) So this year you are going to ask mom before anyone asks you the same question again. (INNIATIVE). "Mom, why do we cut the ends off the ham?" Her answer, "because the oven was too small for a ham to fit into it so we had to cut the ends off to fit." (Realize the need for change of habits)

Develop every Aspect of your life.

Challenge Conventional Thinking

Get out of that comfort zone because it's holding you back from your potential to be great and achieve the success you truly want. To sum it up, self-evaluate the total essence of oneself which is your Thoughts, Health, and Faith or as one would say, your mind, body, and spirit.

Chapter Insight

Success by means of Perception – Story of Two Cajun Friends

Boudreaux had a pick-up truck that he put up for sale. When his friend Thibodeaux asked why he is was selling it, he replies "it's because dat truck got too many of dem miles." After trying to sell the truck for a couple of weeks, Thibodeaux tells him to roll back the odometer to fifty thousand miles and it will sell faster.

About a week later Thibodeaux sees Boudreaux cleaning the truck and packing up for a vacation. He asks Boudreaux, "you got trouble wit dat pick-up sellin?" Boudreaux replies, "Why should I sell? It only got fifty thousand of dem miles."

Moral of the story is that Boudreaux changed something about his daily life, "Perception." He bought into change and decided to embrace a new lifestyle and a new way of thinking. In our daily lives we have to change our perception on how we carry ourselves, how we do business, how we treat others, and most importantly, what it takes to be successful.

Chapter Assignment

Capture the best understanding you can this upcoming week when dealing with situations. View the results in a positive light rather than a negative one. Let's begin to change our perception and do what's necessary to become successful.

PESEVERANCE

"Many of Life's failures are experienced by people who did not realize how close they were to success when they gave up." – Thomas Edison

- Have you ever had an idea of wanting to create something, but you never followed through with it?
- Do you find yourself giving up on things in life because of uncertainty or pessimism?
- To sum things up, sometimes you simply feel like Why me?

Let's first begin by recognizing that you are solely responsible for your OWN DESTINY

Your success can be achieved simply by how you utilize your time management skills, and as a reminder, time waits for no one.

Learn how to Appreciate the Value of Time

Value of a Week

Begin by setting small goals that you can achieve from

week to week, or even set daily goals. They can even be hourly goals.

Value of a Month

Set benchmarks. Be honest with yourself and grade your progress every 1-3 months.

Value of a Year

If you are doing the same thing next year that you are doing right now... Yep you guessed it, chances are you're not growing.

Keep this thought in mind, when your burning desire for success is greater than your deepest fear of failure, you can create anything in your life. Sometimes you need to start from failure to achieve success.

Chapter Assignment

I want to encourage you to create a personal vision statement that will develop a strategic plan for where you want to head in life. Consider making it clear and concise, realistic, and with conviction of why it will motivate you. Also, take into consideration a video diary to help you monitor your progress.

FAILURE

"Nothing in this world is Impossible, the word itself says I'm Possible."   – Audrey Hepburn

Let that sink in for a moment and allow me to share a couple examples about Successful Failures

- Walt Disney was fired as a newspaper editor because he simply had no good ideas.
- Beethoven was told by one of his instructors… "You are hopeless as a composer."
- Sam Walton was told by executives of the Ben Franklin chain, "your ideas for a discount store are not workable."

Don't ever be Afraid to Fail

Embrace the Unknown

The one common denominator the previous examples had in common was incredible attitude - an attitude that "I CAN" and a belief that they could overcome the odds.

Stay Determined and always fail forward

Things Happen

Adversity presents itself quite often but it's how you deal with that adversity that measures your character. It's not what they are doing to me, but what are they doing for me.

In Chapter 1, I mentioned your life doesn't get better by chance it gets better by change. We've all have had moments in our lives that made us feel like we've failed along the way, but somehow, we managed to succeed. Things do happen for a reason, but usually as a result of your actions. Start applying that lesson learned to prevent future mishaps.

Become a Successful Failure

You Determine Your Level of Success

As I mentioned earlier, nothing is impossible, the word itself says I'm Possible. I started my first business back in 2007. I used every saved penny, 401k, IRA, loans, etc. I slept on the couch in my office the entire first year, I joined a gym so that I could shower, and I worked three jobs seven days a week, 12-16-hour days because I was determined not to fail. I told myself, I'M POSSIBLE. I grew a very successful business over a 10-

year period now my purpose is to help GROW YOU.

Chapter Assignment

Stop allowing failure to become a hindrance and view it as a valuable lesson learned to fuel your growth process. Find 3 people to interview/research (someone other than those mentioned) who have made success out of failure.

RESPONSIBILITY

"You must take responsibility. You cannot change the circumstances, the seasons, or the wind, but you can change yourself." — Jim Rohn

What exactly is Responsibility?

Your Personal Obligation

Let's examine the word itself. It can be identified as the ability to choose your response to a situation. You can't blame circumstance for your lack of success or your current situation in life. The price of Greatness is Responsibility (Winston Churchill).

Since the beginning of this book we've been discussing several topics about achieving success in our daily lives. So, let's begin to embrace the situation by taking full responsibility of the choices we make.

Understand that what comes with Responsibility is also Accountability

Own Your Actions

We all have had tendencies to be afraid of responsibility. "Ninety-nine percent of all failures come from people who have a habit of making excuses." (George Washington Carver)

"Truth is, no one can make you feel inferior without your permission." (Eleanor Roosevelt)

Accountability is everything and it starts with YOU. If you're in management, can you blame someone else if you never presented your expectations or effectively led by example? Can you criticize your kids if you never taught them right from wrong? To sum it up BE ACCOUNTABLE!!

Chapter Assignment

I encourage you prioritize the responsibilities in your lives. What's important vs. not important. What's urgent vs. non-urgent.

	Important (I)	Not Important (NI)
Urgent (U)	**UI**	**NIU**
Not Urgent (NU)	**NUI**	**NUNI**

PROCRASTINATION

"It is not the mountain we conquer, but ourselves."
– Sir Edmond Hillary

Know yourself and what really matters in life, so you can determine how to spend your time.

Develop Time Management Skills

- *Track how you spend your time*

     What you put off for tomorrow could've been done yesterday. A to-do list may seem a little out dated but can be very effective.

- *Sharpen your decision-making skills*

     Be creative and think outside the box

- *Challenge the thoughts that prevent you from completing tasks*

Breakdown that Procrastination Barrier

Get Rid of the Hindrance that Surrounds Your Life

Stop putting things off because the longer you keep delaying it, the more you'll feel like you don't want to be bothered with that task.

Focus on concentration on setting smaller goals to breakdown larger tasks. How do you eat an elephant? Simply one bite at a time.

Avoid panicking by removing phrases such as "I don't feel like doing this." "This is boring" "I work better right before deadlines" "I'm afraid I will fail"

Chapter Assignment

I want to encourage you to prioritize your week on Sunday nights on what you want to accomplish during that week. Evaluate your progress by the next week.

Aspiration

"Cherish your visions and your dreams as they are the children of your soul, the blueprints of your ultimate achievements." — *Napoleon Hill*

Become an Entrepreneur in your Own Life

CEO of Self University

Entrepreneurs don't let things happen to them, they MAKE things happen for them.

If you have big goals in life, INVEST in yourself. Take some classes, meditate, exercise more often because these simple short-term investments will create good habits and net you long-term gains.

Own every aspect of your life.

Strengthen your Infrastructure

Each week I leave you with the motto "Sometimes we can't control the cards we are dealt in life, but we can control the outcome." Start by taking back control and do so by taking personal responsibility, creating your vision, and persevering through hardships.

Just when you think your situation is bad, someone else always has it worse. God would never put anything more on you than you can handle. You have to decide when it's time to stop digging a deeper hole for yourself and began working towards solutions to come out of that hole.

Chapter Assignment

I want you to aspire to be GREAT. Create that expectation for yourself because no one else will. Simply take control of your thoughts and actions.

BARRIERS

*"When one door of happiness closes, another opens,
but often we look so long at the closed door that we do
not see the one that has opened for us."*
— Helen Keller

Created Barriers

Be Yourself and Not Like Others

Self-esteem issues, negative environments, current
financial position, maybe you don't have the job or
relationship you desire? These situations and more can
be potential barriers that hinder our growth process.

Tearing down Barriers

Steps Toward Creating a New You

Good news for all of us is that barriers in life can be
torn down, but it takes persistence and determination,
which are key components. Believe that nothing will
hold back as you're determined to reach that end goal.

Building New Foundations

You are the Master of Your Fate

Unlock the full potential of your mind and how it works. Knowing yourself is the first step in challenging yourself to become a better person. Don't take things so personally, but yet grow from the experience.

Chapter Assignment

Identify things that you feel are holding you back. Understand and believe that any obstacle in your path only creates opportunities on the other side of it. Whatever the circumstance you must work on not allowing it to become a threat in your life. If pulling back from family and friends is a way to regain some peace of mind, then you know what you must do.

EXCUSES

"The only reason we don't have what we want in life is the reasons we create why we can't have them."
— Tony Robbins

Living in Fear

Follow Your Gut Feelings

Failure is an easy task - just don't try. Fear will always sabotage our efforts. A lot of people in this world fear the unknown and will make every excuse not to proceed, but later in life will develop "could've, would've, should've" blues. Sometimes you just have to leap.

Embrace Fear

Your Opinion Matters

If you really want to do something in your personal life or professional career, you'll find a way no matter the cost. Don't be afraid to tell others "no" and most importantly stop telling yourself that you can't.

Excuses

Daily Affirmation

Tell yourself when you begin to doubt your actions excuses are monuments of nothingness that builds bridges that lead to nowhere, those who use these tools of incompetence are masters of nothingness.

Chapter Assignment

Find something that motivates you to keep going. It can be personal happiness, kids, or a simple positive affirmation. Create a vision board to look at or something you can read every morning you wake that will give you a sense of purpose.

PEACE OF MIND

"If you are not willing to risk the usual, you will settle for the ordinary." — Jim Rohn

The problems that we encounter from time to time are simply based on our decision-making process. Most of the time the wrong decision will lead to high levels of stress. People make decisions based only on the knowledge they have at the time.

In order to achieve the things, we want out of life we must improve upon our mental processes:

Become a Better Communicator

Read more and learn how to listen effectively to what's not being said. Don't always be ready for a reply as to say you know what the other person is going to ask. At the very moment, you stop listening.

Attention to Detail

Focus your mind and attention to detail and cultivate a positive outlook to any problem or situation.

Seek Inspiration

Inspire your mind through stimulating fun activities to reduce stress levels. Take a trip, exercise more often, or get a massage. Meditation can be a great way to seek inspiration from a higher source.

Chapter Assignment

Get out of that ordinary space and find a place that makes you happy.

PATIENCE

"Patience is not simply the ability to wait, it's how we behave while we're waiting." — Joyce Meyer

Understand your Frustrations

Understanding Self

You may very well be the problem when dealing with others; people that you find to be difficult because they are different in your eyes and don't always agree with your values. Understand that personality, values, beliefs, gender, etc. play a role in effective communication and if you're not willing to open your mind and accept it, the problem with patience lies within oneself.

Give Difficult People a Chance

Learn how to talk their language and respect how they feel. I truly believe you'll get much further in life if you learn how to humble yourself and your actions towards others. You don't have to come to their level but find a common denominator to build on.

Develop Patience for the Right Situation

Accept that We are All Different

How do we exactly accomplish this? First, let's develop an open mind. You're going to have your personal beliefs as well as the other person has his/her. Why waste precious time and unnecessary effort arguing a point of irrelevance when it was easy to just agree to disagree. Secondly, let's improve upon communication lines. That other individual's perception is reality to them, so who are we to judge?

Chapter Assignment

Understand that things hardly go as planned. Patience should be practiced more often, in order to develop it consciously. It has been documented that having patience has bred success, wealth, opportunities, etc. If you plant a tree, it may be years before it bears fruit. Opening a new business, you may not see a profit until months or even years. Plant your seeds in life, cultivate it and through time it'll produce everything you desire.

SELF-CONCEIT

"Try not to become a man of success, rather become a man of value." — *Albert Einstein*

Sometimes You are the Reason you're held back

What does your comfort zone look like? Are you comfortable with your life accomplishments? Are you concerned about what other's opinions are of you? These things or a lack thereof can and will sabotage your success. Don't ever get too wrapped up into self and fail to realize that your selfish ways are the primary reason for stagnation. It's always good to step out of your comfort zone, but don't become so comfortable that you are not willing to try something new.

Convert Self-Conceit into Self-Confidence

No one likes an egotistical individual who views themselves higher than everyone else or one who is always bragging about what they have. Individuals who come across as never doing any wrong or their accomplishments are far greater than yours. Usually the loudest person in the room is the first to make a fool of themself. You never want to be that person, but you do want to build up your confidence. Start by humbling yourself and your actions. Set the precedent for others to want to follow you rather than mock you.

Focus on the following steps to help boost your self-confidence levels:

- Consistently remind yourself of personal successes
- Visualize being successful
- Learn from your mistakes, but don't allow them to hold you back
- Set benchmarks to your goals to help you stay on track

Chapter Assignment

Self-Conceit can be a barrier to your personal growth. Focus on creative ways to tear down to tear down that barrier. Ask family/friends what they truly think of you and use that as a starting point to becoming a better YOU.

Positive Attitude/Environment

"Cherish your visions and your dreams as they are the children of your soul, the blueprints of your ultimate achievements."   – Napoleon Hill

Change Your Way of Thinking

Avoid the FFA – Friends, Family, and Associates Trap

It's proven that when you surround yourself with positive people within positive environments, it always equals positive results. How many times have you found yourself in a situation wanting to improve your life? Let's say you decided you wanted to go back to school, or you wanted a better job paying more money, or you wanted a better relationship. You tell those who you think have your best interest at heart, but that family or friend always managed to say something negative or discouraging that happened to fuel your thoughts of doubt and fear. Truth is, whether a family member or your best friend from high school, if they truly have your best interest they will support you. If they discourage you, it may be time to surround yourself with positive people.

Think Outside the Box

Be Creative

Always think positive; rather than complain do your best to concentrate on the positive elements of the situation. There's always a silver lining in every negative situation, so stop complaining and start seeking.

Hit the reset Button

Recharge as Needed

Create an environment that best suits you and reward yourself quite often. Consider this example, we've all participated in a sports activity at some point in our lives. Whether playing in a peewee league or on a professional level, those activities taught us about life to some degree. When we competed, we had to rely on teammates to help reach that one ultimate goal, which was to win. In life we sometimes have to rely on teammates that consist of family/friends, significant others, and coworkers to conjure a positive environment and share positive attitudes in order to grow effectively. FFA's can also be positive minded people, just be able to distinguish the difference.

Chapter Assignment

Focus your mind and attention on things in your life where you lack confidence and surround yourself with like-minded people. Secondly, read literature that promotes positive thoughts. Finally, BELIEVE IN YOURSELF!

NEGATIVE ATTITUDE

"Opportunities don't happen. You create them."
— Chris Grosser

Importance of Not Thinking Negative Thoughts

Affecting your Confidence

A lack of optimism and character will most definitely result in a lack of confidence. A negative attitude puts you at a disadvantage to succeed at what you desire to accomplish. Never stop believing in your abilities, even when the ones closest to you may have. Reassure yourself daily that I will not be defeated by a lack of confidence.

Build Morale within Yourself

Value your Confidence

Zig Ziglar once quoted, "Your attitude, not your aptitude, will determine your altitude." It doesn't matter how much knowledge you obtain in your lifetime, if you don't carry the right attitude, you'll never go any further in your quest for excellence than right in front of you.

Be Responsible

Accept Responsibility

Accept responsibility for your own actions before you challenge others to do the same. People are always looking at you to practice what you preach, so always try to lead by example.

Daily Affirmation

Keep your thoughts positive
Because your thoughts become
YOUR WORDS

Keep your words positive
Because your words become
YOUR BEHAVIOR

Keep your behavior positive
Because your behavior becomes
YOUR HABITS

Keep your habits positive
Because your habits become
YOUR VALUES

Keep your values positive
Because your values become
YOUR DESTINY

Mahatma Gandhi

Chapter Assignment

Go through your phone book and evaluate the people in your life, both past and present. Purge the negativity if necessary, but be the CHANGE you desire.

NEGATIVE ENVIRONMENTS

"Don't be afraid to give up the good to go for the GREAT." — John D. Rockefeller

Don't allow Yourself to become Stagnant

Avoid at all Cost

What motivates you? Is it self-gratification, happiness, money, or even respect? Focus on your self-development so that you won't get left behind attempting to motivate others. At minimum, give people a chance for they may not know where they're going or how to get there. The biggest issue for stagnation is that we lack the "How To" but instead of surrounding ourselves with a mentor who can teach us the how, we waste our time with those who are comfortable where they are in life.

Lead by Example and Keep Moving Forward

Don't Look for Sympathy

Nobody in this world owes you anything, but yet you are entitled to the things most desirable and you work hard for. Your purpose in life should be to lead by example regarding your family, on the job if you're in management, and those who genuinely look up to you. Learn to choose your battles in life wisely, due to some are easily won and lost by intelligent decisions or a lack thereof. Understand that sometimes people are in the situations they are in for a reason and their reasons shouldn't become yours. When you continuously help the same person out of the same situation and they keep going back, walk away and stop enabling them. They'll eventually realize it's time to stop digging the same hole and learn how to come up out of that situation.

Surround Yourself with Those of Like Attainment

Seek Optimism and Rid Your Thoughts of Pessimism

Nothing is more refreshing than surrounding yourself with individuals who are optimistic about specific tasks and just life in general. Have you ever found yourself in a situation where the group is always gossiping, complaining, sabotaging the efforts of everyone? How did you feel and what approach did you take to deal with the negativity? I've found myself in that situation a few times and simply attempted to shed positive light on the situation or I wound up walking away. You don't need that negative energy in your life especially when you're on the verge of becoming a better YOU.

Chapter Assignment

Begin to encourage individuals you encounter daily who always have a negative perception on life. Share your daily positive affirmations and encourage them to see the big picture.

POSITIVE THINKING

"The most common way people give up their power is by thinking they don't have any."   – Alice Walker

Don't be Afraid to Mimic Successful People

Build Effective Habits

The best, yet easiest way to approach this task is to find a mentor. Once you identify what it is you want out of life, find someone who is highly successful and utilize him or her as your mentor. Mentors are those who have traveled the same roads you are embarking upon and can offer advice that will encourage positive thinking. Other methods to build effective habits can be reading literature about success, retaining key information that applies to you, and focusing on listening more effectively. I can guarantee that the common denominator you'll find is that their success began with positive thinking and habits were built around that.

Develop Knowledge and Not Stereotypes

Take a New Approach

Re-evaluate the how you view others because different cultures have a tendency to impact how people feel and how they respond. Let's examine two individuals with two different beliefs or opinions. Arguing about who is right will do nothing more than waste time, because by the end of the conversation you both will feel the same, but with elevated heart rates. Rather than go through that trouble, just open your mind and listen so that you can learn more about a topic you may be ignorant about. Attempt to read more about current affairs and absorb some cultural things outside of your own.

Cultivate Mental Toughness

Change Your Perspective on Life

Start grasping new ideas and try not to view them as potential threats. Expand your imagination because positive thinking can boost confidence, optimism, and enthusiasm. Lastly, listen to your intuition because it will never steer you wrong. Don't cloud your mind with things of no substance or value. Your brain is a very complex organ and capable of anything you challenge yourself to do. Don't be afraid to go the extra mile because it'll be the difference between mediocrity and greatness.

Chapter Assignment

Challenge yourself to do something different. Be open-minded about the experience and keep a positive attitude. You may be surprised by the outcome based off you changing your thought process.

DISCOURAGEMENT

"Beating yourself up doesn't benefit anyone. Focus on what you choose to create instead."

Change the way You do Things

Life Requires Planning

Plan ahead for the change you want to see in your life. Think both in the short-term as well as in the long-term. Your short-term objectives are going to serve as stepping-stones to get you where you ultimately want to be in life. A few examples to utilize are to determine who you are as an individual. What's your purpose and mission in life? A lot of us don't know what our purpose is and spend a lifetime trying to figure it out. Where do you ultimately want to be in life? Create a vision board with your goals and objectives and review daily. Finally, create a bucket list and go for it. You enjoyed your childhood years, work for 30+ years, only to look forward to retirement to pursue your list and enjoy life again. Enjoy life each and every day and don't be afraid to push limits.

Be Open-Minded to New Concepts/Ideas

Remedy for Discouragement

Discouragement happens to all of us; most of the time it's difficult to overcome because we don't want to deal with the situation directly or whatever consequences that may come along. Always be honest with yourself and stop pretending that things don't bother you. You can't take action against negative feelings until you admit you have them. There's a connection between mind/body/emotions so you have to take care of body to prevent things such as stress, poor health, and esteem issues. Always make sure you mature from your mistakes so that you won't continue to take the same actions that haven't been working.

Focus on Your Future rather than Living in Your Past

Can't Receive the New holding onto the Old

Think about every vehicle you have ever driven in your lifetime. Have you ever wondered why your front windshield is larger than the back? First and foremost, the concept of driving requires you to look ahead and not behind. Think of the front windshield as being your outlook to endless opportunities ahead of you, so we have to continue to push towards them. Although you sometimes turnaround and look through back windshield, your attention should be focused on what's in front of us and not behind. The purpose of the rearview mirror is to simply remind us from where we came, but the ultimate goal is to get where we are going.

Chapter Assignment

We all have tendencies to get discouraged when we feel that things are not going our way. For this assignment I want you to identify what hasn't worked in the past and why? Come up with refreshed ideas to achieve your goals. I'm certain for most people, once discouragement hit they never revisited that situation.

Unrealistic Expectations

*"Ninety-nine percent of all failures come from people
who have a habit of making excuses."*
– George Washington Carver

Fun Facts

George Washington Carver was born in 1864 as a slave and went on to become a world-famous chemist that made important discoveries and inventions to help revolutionize the world. His research on peanuts, soybeans, sweet potatoes, pecans, and other products helped poor southern farmers vary their crops and improve their diets. He found solutions to restore nutrients to the soil by rotating crops, and he set out to change lives and helped shape the world. As mentioned in the above quote, GWC didn't make a habit of making excuses. The goals he achieved may have been unrealistic to most people, but they were not to him. He found something he loved and as a result of hard work, he came to be recognized as one of the great inventors in this world.

Others Beliefs in Us

Family/Friends Opinions

Often times, over-expectations that others carry for us can be detrimental to our mental psyche. They expect you to succeed, always giving you additional unnecessary feedback; don't believe you're capable of failing, but the reality of it is, you are human. I'm sure those expectations are only designed to motivate you to be great, but sometimes they can be too unrealistic. Those unrealistic expectations affect our personal relationships, shut down our personal goals, and even steer our lives in opposite directions. Too many times, people try to live their dreams through you, and not allow you to live your own.

Create Opportunities

Make Things Happen for You

Just because you think you're deserving of something doesn't necessarily mean you're entitled to it. You have to make things happen and it begins by putting in the hard work to go get it. If you expect to fail, the battle is already lost. Instead, believe in yourself that you can achieve any and everything.

Chapter Assignment

Start setting real goals and expectations for yourself as well as others around you. If you want someone to be great, allow him or her to be that. Offer up motivation and inspiration, but don't attempt to dictate their goals and aspirations.

UNREALISTIC GOAL SETTING

"You measure the size of the accomplishment by the obstacles you had to overcome to reach your goals."
– Booker T. Washington

Develop Resources

A goal is unrealistic when the goal is something that requires more energy, skills, talents and time than you have available in order to achieve it. (Lara Honos-Webb, PhD.) We can accomplish anything we set our minds to, we just need to develop our skills and become more enthusiastic towards achieving that specific set of goals. Reading more, developing hobbies, going back to school, learning a new trade, and networking can all be forms of resources to help grow you as an individual.

Importance of REAL Goals

Stop Setting the Bar Too High

When you set the bar to high, you are only sabotaging your greatness. Let's examine relationships; we want what we desire but it's rare you'll find every single characteristic in that other person you're looking for. Do we truly find our soul mates, or we simply find individuals that we can tolerate? Usually, we put so much time and effort into something that we don't want to start over. I use to tell my female students when it comes to relationships, stop setting the bar too high to where a man can't ever meet your expectations, but then don't set too low where he can easily stumble upon exceeding them by mistake. If that other person finds value within you, they will work towards meeting your goals and expectations, so know your worth.

When we set realistic goals that are attainable, it will only help boost your self-esteem, personal happiness, and our overall wellbeing.

Chapter Insight

Imagine yourself on a path towards success. The end goal may be a promotion, college degree, a successful business, etc. On one side of the road are dreams/fantasies and on the other side of the road is reality. In order to get to that goal at the end of the path, you must remain focused. Along that path to success, life presents us with obstacles in the form speed bumps, hurdles, etc. Yet with all that around us, you should still be determined to get to the finish line.

You could lose focus and spend too much time with dreams in a fantasy world; reality will quickly bring you to that side of the road and slap you in the face. The obstacles you face can also come in the form of negative people, with negative attitudes, within negative environments that will always attempt to discourage you. But if you stay the course, have faith, believe and see yourself achieving that goal, that prize is yours. Building and maintaining healthy relationships will also help you achieve this feat. Those who are there for you and share a like attainment to succeed, will help push, pull to keep you upright and even carry you over a few hurdles.

Chapter Assignment

Start setting simple and small goals to achieve daily and weekly. Once you get into the habit of consistently following up, start focusing on bigger goals to shoot for.

S.M.A.R.T. GOALS

"You measure the size of the accomplishment by the obstacles you had to overcome to reach your goals."
– Booker T. Washington

Develop sound goals to help develop your Life

Why not have goals so big, you feel uncomfortable telling small-minded people? Those who lack vision will probably never understand greatness until they change their way of thinking. Never tell pessimistic people your goals and dreams because their negativity will usually create negative vibes and attempt to discourage you. Instead, quietly move about things, accomplish those goals and proceed to lead by example.

Complete the following example:

LIFE POKER SMART GOAL WORKSHEET

Start Date: _____ Target Date: _____

Goal:

_____

_____

Specific: What exactly will you accomplish?

_____

_____

_____

_____

_____

_____

_____

Measurable: How will you know when you have reached this goal?

_____

_____

_____

_____

_____

_____

_____

Achievable: Is achieving this goal realistic with effort and commitment? Have you got the resources to achieve this goal? If not, how will you get them?

_____

_____

_____

_____

_____

_____

_____

Relevant: Why is this goal significant to your life?

_____

_____

_____

_____

_____

_____

_____

Timely: When will you achieve this goal?

_____

_____

_____

_____

_____

_____

Why is this goal(s) important?

_____

_____

_____

The benefits of achieving this goal(s) will be:

_____

_____

_____

_____

_____

_____

Potential Obstacles   **Potential Solutions**

_____   _____

_____   _____

_____   _____

Specific Action Steps: What steps need to be taken to get you to your goal?

What?	Expected Completion Date	Completed
_____	_____	_____
_____	_____	_____

Chapter Assignment

Utilize the template to create multiple SMART goals to help shape and change your Life. Go back to Chapter 8 – Perseverance where we talked about the value of time. Make sure the goals you pursue are time sensitive.

DESIRE/PASSION

"Persistence can change failure into extraordinary achievement." – Matt Biondi

Love What You Do

Be Enthusiastic

You should always be enthusiastic about life, you did wake up this morning when someone else didn't. Appreciate your ability to wake up every single morning and have an opportunity to make a difference. How many times have you awakened and told yourself with disgust, ugh I'm going to have a bad day. Funny thing is you hadn't even gotten up out the bed, but yet you managed to speak that into existence, which led to that bad day. Be enthusiastic about the things you want in life. When you arise each morning, thank God first, and then speak of how great of a day you're going to have. Every day is a new chance for you to create exciting opportunities in your life. When you get excited about things, you most certainly will always put your best foot forward. Sometimes you have to do the things you don't want to do, in order to get to where you want to be in life.

Feed Your Cravings for Success

Desire to be GREAT

Ask yourself what it is you desire personally. What exactly is desire? Desire is something that brings satisfaction and enjoyment into one's life. We often desire things that add no value to our lives but run from the desired things that require hard work and persistence. Long-term failure will result when you consistently make excuses instead of decisions. Make the decisions that will add value, then passionately pursue them. The only thing waiting for you will be other successful people.

Chapter Insight

I often get asked how did I achieve my current level of success, or even sometimes asked to serve as a business mentor? I usually respond with a short story, particularly my personal story of success. Some are intrigued, engaged, and a few may even lose interest. By the end of the story, most are excited and motivated, yet a few will follow up by saying, I hear you but how did you get to this point of success. I realized that those who didn't care to listen lacked desire and passion. They want to skip the hard work component and jump right into success. Those who were engaged took from it, in order to be successful, I have to be passionate about what I do every day and remain humble. The CEO of Walmart started out working as a truck un-loader. He worked himself from the ground up in high school to now, all because he had desire and passion.

Chapter Assignment

What humble beginnings story will you share to inspire others? You may not be the CEO of a major corporation, but you can impact other people's lives based on your life. Start re-shaping your life to become an inspiration to others.

TEMPTATION

> *"I am not a product of my circumstances. I am a product of MY decisions."*   – Stephen Covey

Limit Distractions in Your Life

Stop Being Enticed by Negative People

I mentioned earlier, it's easy to get distracted but even harder to get back on track. Some of the circles you frequent, have and will always be around, so I want you to start listening to what's not being said. Negative people love to gossip and if you don't pay attention, they'll pull you right in with them, followed by throwing you under the bus as if you made the comments. Sound familiar? Another example are media outlets, we get distracted by foolishness in the media daily, but don't pay attention to what's going on behind the scenes. We get sucked into things that are irrelevant and fail to focus on things that will improve your quality of life.

Temptation Comes in Many Forms

Don't Eat the Cheese

People will attempt to discourage any chance they get, so stop allowing individuals rent space inside of your head for free. They will tempt you with words to pull you out of character and try to get you to prove something. Temptation will present itself in the form of money, power, respect, sex, but all it does is provides you with temporary pleasures. You find yourself wanting more of the tempting pleasures, only to find lack of love, self-respect, wealth, and empowerment, which are the building blocks to building a strong a character.

Chapter Assignment

Focus on your needs and what's important for your success. Stop trying to compete with others and live like the Joneses. When you start to accept and appreciate what you have, only then will bigger and better things come into your life.

INTEGRITY/TRUTH

"Never give in except to convictions of honor and good sense."   *– Winston Churchill*

Never Abandon Your Morals

Your Character is Every Thing

Begin to do what is best for self and not what's best for everyone else. Don't ever give up your right to be wrong because you can lose your ability to meet new people and learn new things. The objective is to simply keep moving forward. As you grew from a child into adulthood, you were always taught the difference between right and wrong. Your parents and teachers armed you with the necessary tools in your toolbox to utilize in life. It's always been up to you to keep those tools sharpened and to know when to use them in the right situation.

Develop Better Principles in Your Life

Be Honest with Yourself First and Foremost

Sometimes you have to look yourself in the mirror and

bite the bullet. If you can't be honest with yourself, you can't expect to be that way with others. We all want others to be biased with us, cosign on what we want to hear and not give the direct truths, but that's not helping your character. It's not what other people think about you, but what you think about yourself is all that matters. Although truth can sometimes hurt, it's still what is always needed.

Chapter Assignment

Is there ever such a thing as an honest man? I'm sure it would take a lifetime to seek out such a person especially when you can't even look in the mirror and be honest with self. If you are in constant denial, you have some real soul searching to do. I challenge you to identify your weaknesses and begin to create solutions to strengthen them.

"Real integrity is doing the right thing, knowing that nobody's going to know whether you did it or not." – *Oprah Winfrey*

Giving Up

"Nobody's perfect, we all fall down. What matters most is how quickly we get back up, learn from our mistakes and move on."

Simply Get Things Done

Focus on Outcome

You'll be amazed at what you can accomplish if you simply just take action. Lots of people are afraid to jump because of potential and perceived failure. I posed this question to you, how will you ever know if you can fly if you don't spread your wings? Earlier in the book I mentioned you are solely responsible for your own destiny, so you should learn to become more comfortable with self. Your action versus reaction will always determine the outcome of a situation. Remember time waits for no one, thus you should attempt to get it right the first time to avoid repeat. Repeating task will continue to discourage you if it persists.

Beware of Dream Killers

Understand What is Relevant and What is Not

Do individuals who are always talking about seeing the big picture, but they never want to contribute in getting there? They have a tendency to gravitate towards what's irrelevant rather than the important task at hand. They call themselves "so-called" friends, and will gossip, laugh about a friend who is in need of help and guidance, rather than pray for or offer encouragement for them to do better. More than likely, the same "so-called" friends are doing the same thing behind your back when you're not around. People can be very pessimistic and get complacent, which is why they never grow, and quickly to give up on life. Disassociate yourself from that pessimism and focus on what's relevant in your life, because if not, you'll find yourself in the same boat of complacency and settling for less.

Chapter Assignment

The great Vince Lombardi once said, "Perfection is not attainable, but if we chase perfection we can catch excellence." Don't be so quick to give up on ideas, things, and people who are meaningful in your life. We tend to pray for things and the first thing that happens is that we go through a test. The test is not to discourage you or make you give up, but rather make you a stronger individual in regards to what you asked for.

SUCCESS

*"A successful man is one who can lay a firm foundation
with the bricks that others throw at him."*
— David Brinkley

Hard Work + Ambition = SUCCESS

Respect the Grind

The grind is when you're sleeping at night and I'm up late nights working. The grind is pushing yourself to the limit and not giving up. The grind requires sacrifice to give up your wants and pursue your needs. The grind is doing what needs to be done like you really want to do it. When you can accept these things and put in the hard work, only then your success will come. Thomas Edison who had an insane work ethic stated, "Success is 1% inspiration, 99% perspiration."

How do You Measure Success?

It's not always about Money and Power

Some of the richest and most powerful people in this world don't measure their success by how much money or fame they have, their measuring rod consist of core values in which they believe in. We tend to get confused by what others have and don't realize we can have the same things. However, what if you had all the money in the world and it still didn't make you happy? You see famous persons in the news daily self-destructing because they lack personal happiness and overlook the little things in life that matter most. Success can be measured several different ways; it's just a determination of what means most to you. Success can be personal happiness, overall well-being, self-gratification, and peace of mind. There are others, but notice the values that I mentioned, they all have one common denominator which is YOU. When you are completely happy, you will be ultimately successful and make impacts in others' lives. Maya Angelou once stated, "Success is liking yourself, liking what you do, and liking how you do it."

Chapter Insight

THE COST OF AMBITION

- *Late nights, early mornings.*
- *Lots of associates, very few friends.*
- *You will be misunderstood.*
- *You will be single unless you're lucky enough to find someone who understands your lifestyle.*

- *People will want you to do good, but never better than them.*

For these reasons, you will do many things alone.

Chapter Assignment

Define what success means to you and how you are going to be impactful in others' lives each and every day.

OBSTACLES/DISTRACTIONS (WILD CARD)

"Stop chasing the money and start chasing the passion." — Tony Hsieh

Believe that Obstacles Result into Opportunities

Any Road You Take Will Get You There

Setting your priorities in order is always the first step of the journey. Make sure you do things with consistency and always have a plan in addition to alternative methods. Ponder this; doesn't it sometimes seem like no matter how much you plan, something will always go wrong? Or you feel like job opportunities are missed based off whom you know? Although this may be true in most instances, you can never allow anything to deter you from your dreams. You've heard the phrase, "step out on faith" before. Ask yourself, what do I have to lose by doing so? If you're current process is not working, then you need to grab onto something greater. Have faith in God and have faith in yourself. Whenever you encounter an obstacle know that there's an opportunity waiting for you. If you were told that there was $1 million on the other side of a 12-foot wall, you would attempt everything you could to climb over, go around, or even go through it if needed be. So, if you're willing to expend that much energy, why not expend it on your dreams and aspirations?

Learn How to Deal with Distractions

Avoid the Push and Pull Effect

How many times have you constructed a plan to accomplish a specific task(s) that you wanted to do for self, but someone always managed to push or pull you away from it to do something for them? People may have come to you for simple advice, but then it turned into a social gathering. Understand that most of your problems could be self-inflicted, with such things like day dreaming, easily getting side tracked, or doing the most for others. If any of this sounds familiar, then let me suggest that you stop making excuses as to why you got distracted and change your habits to do better.

Develop Passion for What You Do

Motivate Yourself as Often as Possible

When those feelings of not going anywhere or doing

anything with your life comes about, change the way you do things. You must develop a sense of passion for what you want to do. Whether it's on your job or a personal journey, you have to be excited about what you do day in and day out. The quote at the beginning of the chapter referenced not chasing the money but chase your passion. When you're passionate about something, you'll motivate others to do the same. Have you ever heard of the Pareto principle; commonly known as the 80/20 rule, 80 percent of sales come from 20 percent of customers? How does it apply to your life? Focus on your passion, and the rest will come into your life effortlessly. Work to your strengths to develop your self-awareness, the result is that you'll begin to focus on the positive things and start eliminating the negativity.

Chapter Assignment

I referred to this chapter as the wild card because these things happen every day of our lives. Adversity comes at us many different ways unexpectedly so we shouldn't be so quick to give up. Whenever one door closes, know that there are always other windows of opportunities awaiting you. Focus on the goals in front of you and forget about the distractions behind you.

CONFIDENCE/TAKE ACTION

"Do one thing every day that scares you."
- Mary Schmich

Take the Road Less Traveled

It will make a Difference

Often times, the road less traveled is better than not taking one at all. Stop holding your decision-making hostage because you're afraid of failure. Don't be so indecisive when it comes to what you want to do but find yourself being the biggest cheerleader when it comes to others. Act independently and don't allow others to dictate what you do with their "so-called" opinions. Self-improvement may require you to be different from the pack, so upon deciding what's best for you and/or family will require you taking the path that's best for you.

Don't be a Quitter

Believe in Yourself

Quitters never plan to win and winners never plan to

lose. If you never believe in yourself, how can you expect others to take you seriously? Belief in oneself requires having faith in your abilities. It is important to challenge yourself by digging deep within to conquer those fears. Only then will you become an unstoppable force, but you have to first believe and free yourself from captivity of negative feelings.

Daily Affirmation

<u>INVICTUS</u>

Out of the night that covers me
Black as the Pit from pole to pole
I thank whatever gods maybe
For my unconquerable soul.

In the fell clutch of circumstance
I have not winced nor cried aloud
Under the bludgeoning's of chance
My head is bloody, but unbowed

Beyond this place of wrath and tears
Looms but the Horror of the shade
And yet the menace of the years
Finds, and shall find me unafraid

It matters not how strait the gate

How charged with punishments the scroll
I am the master of my fate
I am the captain of my soul.

By: William Ernest Henley

Chapter Assignment

Identify some confidence builders in your life that will allow you to believe in your ability to be successful. If you have children, maybe it's the idea of leaving a legacy behind to be carried on. You may just want to be impactful in the lives of others, so whatever your desire is, it starts with self-confidence.

ADVERSITY

"Adversity can be turned to opportunity simply by adjusting our perception and our attitude."

Stop Placing Restrictions on Your Expectations

Become Extraordinary

During times of adversity, you must display resiliency no matter what comes about you. Friends will always show their true colors in times of adversity. Adversity can be an indicator to show whose really with you versus those who are not. Even family can contribute to negative situations by being biased rather than being truthful. At some point in our lives we will experience or encounter some adversity in the form of financial hardship, affliction, or relationships. One thing you have the ability to do is turn something negative into something positive. The storms that we endure only occur to make you stronger. Don't ever undervalue yourself, know your worth, and then improve upon it. Improve self through reading books, listening to motivational speakers, and seek to improve your life skills. Be extraordinary when it comes to success.

If You Cannot, Learn How To

Concentrate on Results

If something you do is no longer effective, go back to the drawing board to keep perfecting it until you get it right. View adversity as a wake-up call that challenges you to be great. In order to obtain the best results, your <u>mindset</u> has to be in the right place. Stop making <u>excuses</u> because you're afraid of the unknown. Have <u>faith</u> in God, your abilities, or a higher source greater than you. Stop settling for no as an answer and be <u>persistent</u> in what you're seeking. <u>Energize</u> yourself with each success you encounter, which will help strengthen your foundation for overall success.

Chapter Assignment

Identify causes of adversity that may be holding you back from reaching your goals. Embrace the situation and build new skills to improve in your life each and every day.

DOUBT

"Our doubts are traitors and make us lose the good we oft might win, by fearing to attempt."
– William Shakespeare

Trust Your Intuition

Be Risky

Do you ever find yourself questioning your abilities? You have a tendency to doubt yourself due to failed attempts in the past. Many of the opportunities that come your way will be missed because of that reason alone, so therefore take risk as often as possible. Every risk has a reward, and high risks will yield high rewards. Falling down can sometimes be an accident but staying down is a choice.

Stop being Timid, Start Living Life

Explore New Things & Ideas

You cannot discover new things unless you develop the courage to step forward and embrace life. Living everyday always taking two steps forward and three steps back can be detrimental to your progress. Embrace your destiny now because 5, 10, 20 years from now, you don't want to look back and be disappointed by the things you didn't do. I remember reading an article about a new crypto currency back in 2010. Although it seemed farfetched, I told myself I would purchase a few shares. I never followed through and we've all seen what the market has been doing lately (shaking my head). Although time waits for no one, it is on your side when you develop patience. People fail to make decisions because they allow doubt to creep in, then find themselves regretting later.

Chinese Proverb

"The best time to plant a tree was 20 years ago. The second best time is now."

Chapter Assignment

Trust your instincts, because it usually never steers you wrong. Doubting yourself due to fear of the unknown causes you to second-guess yourself. Once you make an initial decision you feel comfortable with, go with it. The worst that may happen is that it's a mistake made, but there's also an opportunity to learn from it.

STRENGTH

"Every great dream begins with a dreamer. Always remember you have within you the strength, the patience, and the passion to reach for the stars and change the world." — *Harriet Tubman*

Develop Signature Strengths

Strengthen Your Mental Acuity

Work on strengthening your mental toughness as often as possible. Sometimes adversity is the best thing that will ever happen to you in life, and you absolutely don't need another person's approval to make you successful. Criticism should only make you stronger if you're humble enough to receive it. Think about how much of an impact a negatively toxic person can have in your life. That can be quite an influence if you truly respect that person. Whenever you find yourself thinking about things that upset you, practice being grateful to someone else instead. There are plenty individuals who deserve your attention, so don't waste it on those who don't matter.

Be Resilient in Your Actions

Learn how to Adapt

Allow me to share some food for thought. I would rather be completely exhausted from the hard times which breed success, rather than well rested from achieving nothing. Tough times never last, but those who endure their hardships become strong survivors. I'm sure you've questioned yourself a time or two as to why everyone around you has given up, so why don't you? I want to encourage you to never surrender nor succumb to adversity, because if you look at adversity on the lighter side it will only strengthen who you are as a person. You'll find out just how strong you are when you encounter weakness. Therefore, start building your mindset by acknowledging that you can accomplish anything thrown your way. It may take you a little longer to overcome than most but keep hacking away piece by piece. It's ok if you start slow, but always finish strong.

Chapter Assignment

Focus on developing the things that we are great at and begin to create new strengths in the process. Always use available resources and please do not burn bridges. Remember to continue to be resilient, because when you can overcome adversity, you will be one of the most successful persons you've ever known.

Overindulgence

"You only lose what you cling to." – Buddha

Don't be Greedy

Is it worth it?

Being overindulgent can hinder your mind, body, and spirit. It can lead to abnormalities with both health and wealth. You hear things all the time about doing things in moderation, but it's human nature that triggers us to go overboard from time to time. You don't recognize it, but we come across as being selfish when there's more than enough to go around. I have many friends who will tell me daily they live their lives unselfishly, yet I see them perform selfish acts just about every other day. Have you ever wondered why a group of highly successful friends can't come together to create a successful business venture? This generally happens when one or more is always overindulgent, not willing to humble themselves, and wants to be a control freak even when they lack vision and understanding. Being overindulgent only leads to someone making irrational decisions and intoxicating relationships whether professional or personal.

Be Over-Confident vs. Overindulgent

Boost Your Confidence Level

There's a fine line between confidence and cockiness. There's nothing wrong with being confident in your abilities but being over the top can draw unwarranted attention. People love confident leaders and will follow wherever they are led due to that trust factor. Overindulgence can be easily perceived as making a fool of oneself. To avoid, develop yourself in the areas in which you are good at and become an expert in that category. Something about being confident makes you hold your head higher and want to put your best foot forward. Overindulge yourself in gratitude as often as possible because it is fundamental to your peace and happiness. Appreciate what's in front of you and stop fooling yourself by thinking you need something that you don't have in order to be happy. Once you learn to accept the small things in life, you'll then be blessed with new ones.

Chapter Assignment

You never need to be greedy because there's more than enough to go around. Always ask yourself is it worth it? If that answer is yes, be confident in your abilities to accomplish whatever task may come about you.

STRESS

"Your time is limited, so don't waste it living someone else's life. Don't be trapped by dogma – which is living with the results of other people's thinking."
– Steve Jobs

Maintain a Healthy Balance

Regulate Your Thoughts

Within the human body, our survival depends on 11 body systems working together to maintain a relatively constant condition within our internal environment. In medical terms, this concept is referred to as homeostasis. To sum it up, we are in a healthy state when we are balanced and firing on all cylinders. Translation to our everyday lives, in order to maintain a constant state of mind, it simply begins with our thought process. You must change the way you think, view, and conceptualize difficult people and processes. Regulate your thoughts, as being positive and then positive things will almost immediately begin to manifest. Even when you're having the most difficult day, take a step back, begin to think positive, read something inspirational, or even look at persons around and see that your problems may not be as worse as they may seem.

Don't Allow Yourself to be Susceptible to Malignancy

Adapt and Adjust Regularly

To accomplish self-regulation, our bodies deploy a control center system referred to as a negative feedback loop. Example, whenever there is a disturbance from our external environment such as cold weather, your body detects a sudden drop in temperature, followed by your brain signaling your muscles to start shivering to generate heat and warm yourself up. By design, we are able to adapt and adjust as needed to any pleasurable or unpleasant circumstance. Whenever you come in contact with negative people, you should adjust yourself accordingly and not get pulled into the environment. Your intuition will warn you about a negative situation, potential dangers, but you have to learn how to stop being susceptible to nonsense. Another feedback mechanism our bodies experience is called positive feedback, aka the "viscous cycle" or you know it as stress. Most of the stress we experience in our lives comes from people we know and their constant complaining. You don't want to see them hurt, so you take on their problems, but then realize they constantly keep making the same decisions. Limit your stress levels by what you're able to control. The bricks you carry daily should be heavy enough, so stop taking on additional problems that are of no concern to you.

Chapter Assignment

Create a few stress management protocols in your life to limit your stress levels. The following are a few ideas to get you started:

- Reduce demands on your body
- Support healthy lifestyle changes
- Practice relaxation and meditation daily
- Learn how to say "No"

HAPPINESS

"If you want to live a happy life, tie it to a goal, not to people or things." — Albert Einstein

Seek Happiness Constantly

Happiness Inspires Growth

Happiness starts within you. Family, work, friends, pets, etc. can make you overjoyed, yet those same things can bring about a sadness and turn your world upside down. Worrying about things you have no control over will only cause turmoil in your life. Life is all about the choices you make and whether good or bad, you must be willing to deal with both reward and consequences. Those close to you will have the tendency to consistently make bad decisions and lean on you for help. It's ok to empathize with them but be firm when encouraging them to make better decisions in life. Notice I said empathize and not sympathize, there is a distinct difference. You can go over and beyond and be there for everyone else, but how of those same individuals are truly there for you? When you're happy you love hard, you do things with passion, and people flock towards you. A lack of happiness will always sabotage your efforts for being successful. Understand that you are a special person with beautiful characteristics on the inside waiting to radiate on the outside. Make a commitment to be happy the rest of your life by setting attainable goals, continuing to strengthen your support system, and most importantly ACCEPT WHO YOU ARE! God made every one of you in a unique way and He didn't make any mistakes.

You are not an Average Individual

Don't Ignore the Writing on the Wall

One of the first steps in settling for less is a sense of feeling obligated. You never want to tell others no, but when you consistently submit yourself by saying yes, you allow yourself to become an enabler. People will consistently play on your emotions if you allow them. Relationships are always both difficult and challenging at the same time. Sometimes people grow apart or fall out of love and when you've been in relationship for so long, you start to settle and make excuses as to why you'll stay in something that makes you miserable. Maybe you've been in something for so long, you simply don't want to start over again, and the result, you've settled once again. What does your comfort zone look like? Are you satisfied with your accomplishments in life? Are you concerned about what others' perceptions are of you? Don't ever get wrapped up into these things and fail to realize you are the primary reason for your lack of happiness.

Chapter Assignment

Identify the things that make you happy in your life. Dedicate time and effort into what satisfies you and not beneficial to others. There's nothing wrong with helping others, but when you stop doing for self, your happy meter will fall.

PAIN

"Pain is temporary. It may last a minute, or an hour, or a day, or a year, but eventually it will subside or something else will take its place. If I quit, however it lasts forever." – Lance Armstrong

Understand what Triggers You

Pay Attention to Your Emotions

There are many forms of pain that affect us and can be considered an inevitable part of our lives. Pain can be associated with many things such as, disappointment, traumatic experiences, and the loss of a loved one. Pain can result in unhealthy methods to try and comfort yourself by way of overeating, drugs, and alcohol, or sometimes even depression. Instead, pay attention to your thoughts and feelings in order to get to the center of your mental anguish. I remember when my grandmother passed away and during that time it was a very stressful time in my life. To see one of your loved ones who was the rock of your family go through what she endured. I saw a strong woman who retired early in order to take care of her sister who had cancer, only to succumb to the same fate years later. During that time, I learned an important trait and that was endurance. Although, my grandmother suffered physically, she never gave into pain mentally or emotionally. She even stopped taking pain medications the final year of her life. Here I was an emotional wreck, as would anyone in that position, but I had to understand how to cope with my emotions. That entire situation taught me about endurance, that I could overcome any situation that came my way. The storms we endure are only temporary, so there's no need to let pain plague mind and body.

Take Action in Your Life

Find New Things to Occupy Yourself

Always allow yourself to grieve so that you can begin to overcome pain. Take action by seeking help from those who are positive. It's ok to open up to people and new ideas; it will help increase your accountability. Strengthen the current support systems you have in place and ask them for feedback often. Volunteer your time to help a worthy cause or individual because it will allow you to develop new skills and opportunity to meet a diversity of new people. Most importantly it will help boost your self-esteem and personal development.

Chapter Assignment

Enjoy Life! Get moving and learn how to relax as deemed necessary. Whether it is exercise or meditating, step outside of your comfort zone as often as possible so that you don't find yourself focusing on pain. Whatever your plan maybe, create the plan, implement it, monitor your actions, and make adjustments along the way.

LOVE/FAITH

"Better to have loved and lost than to have never loved at all." — *St. Augustine*

Love the Powerful Emotion

Love is Action

Love is not always about individual self, but about those around us that we endear. Love is the creative ability to see the need before the need even occurs. In other words, it's an empathetic heartfelt concern to meet the need of someone before they discover they're within a need. Often times we let love, the emotion, get the best of us, rather than allow love the action to kick in and take control of our current situations. In regards to your professional life, if you are not doing what you love, then you are wasting your time. We're only here to learn to love.

Foundation of Faith

Confidence, Belief, Assurance

Faith is the foundation of things you prayed for, hoped

for, and believed in. It is the hope that is leveled by reality yet allows you to be optimistic about the impossible. With faith we can't naturally see, but what you feel is manifested within the Spirit of God. Faith is your ability to be grateful even when what you initially hoped for never manifested. Your confidence, beliefs, and assurance are celebrated on the premise that what you had initially hoped for and wanted to come to pass in reality, you are happier than what you would been initially had it came into fruition because you were spared from something you did not see coming that may have been detrimental.

Chapter Insight - *Story of Unwavering Faith*

Two frogs inside a burning house; both had faith, but as the first frog screamed, Oh Lord help... He stayed put. The second frog screamed Oh Lord help, but he then attempted to jump saying Oh Lord during each leap. The first frog burned with the home, while the second frog escaped. Moral of the story is faith without works is dead. Sometimes we pray for God's help and when He answers, we expect Him to do all the work and deliver. You can ask for a new house, He'll bless you with the materials to build one, but you looking for the house to already be built and fall in your lap. Reality is that when you ask for something, when He answers, you still have to put forth some effort in order for it to completely manifest.

Chapter Assignment

As I mentioned you have to love what you do in order to be successful. You must show that affection towards the people you truly care about as much as possible. Whenever you pray and ask God for something, have faith that it will come to pass. Often we get blessed with it, but it requires a little action on our part. We become lazy and want it to fall directly into our laps. You may pray for a new house but then get blessed with the materials. You fail to realize that you were blessed to build the house you want, rather than one that's complete and may cause you problems. Remain faithful and love what you do and the rest will take care of itself.

PRAYER

"Yesterday is history, tomorrow is a mystery, today is a gift from God, which is why we call it the present."
— Bill Keane

Power of Prayer

Have an Open Communication Line

Prayer is that vehicle that carries your inner thoughts, concerns, and questions. Don't concern yourself with man and his opinion; all you have to do is be yourself before God Almighty. I've always heard the saying; man doesn't have a heaven or a hell to put you in. Prayer is God's way of comfort and it is guidance into the path of righteousness.

Prayer Changes Things

Prayer is Your Lifeline

Whenever you need direction or guidance in life, instead of asking Siri© where to go, ask God. His word will illuminate within you, then you will be able to understand His workings with, for, and through your life. Don't look back at yesterday's disappointments, but always look ahead to God's promises that are yet to unfold in your life.

Chapter Assignment

Take some time out of your day and say a prayer with sincerity. It may come in the form of meditation daily, but whatever it is, the key is to focus on the higher source.

Emotional Distress

"If you don't design your own life plan, chances are you'll fall into someone else's plan. And guess what they have planned for you? Not much." — *Jim Rohn*

Don't Hold onto Nonsense

Self-Love is Key

Learn how to walk away from people or things that no longer serve a positive purpose in your life. You allow guilt and sympathy to hinder you from making tough decisions, which in the end only leaves you feeling empty on the inside. You may not be where you want to be in life, someone may not love you anymore, there may even be people around you doubting your abilities, or you may just feel like other people's lives are better than yours. None of those previous examples really matter if you don't start loving yourself.

Don't ever settle for less than what you deserve because you deserve the best. One misconception is that every person and every situation may not always be working against you. You ideally see things the way you perceive your reality to be, so your level of success may be different than that of your counterpart. You may have an introvert personality vs. an extrovert or committed to something or someone else. Whatever the scenario, focus on self-love now so that you avoid emotional distress later.

Become the Bigger Person

Forgive, Forget, Forbear

Forgiveness is always better than holding onto pain and empty feelings. Being a bigger person in any situation shows maturity and growth within you. You shouldn't have to argue all the time, especially regarding petty things. Your communication has broken down at this point, so instead open your mind to see things from the other person's point of view. Build upon your self-confidence by forgiving yourself and stop blaming others.

Forgive yourself for the mistakes you've made by letting go your past. Forgive those that hurt you the most in your life. You can never go backwards, only forward in life. You can't change yesterday, but we can determine tomorrow.

Chapter Assignment

Surround yourself with positive people daily because negative individuals will drain you mentally, physically, and emotionally. They will want you to do better, but never better than them.

RESPECT (WILD CARD)

"The question isn't who is going to let me, it's who is going to stop me."   *– Ayn Rand*

Develop Self-Respect

Identify What Respect Means to You

How do you present yourself daily? What do you see when you look into the mirror? Do you have a sense of pride and confidence about yourself? How do you think others perceive you? All of these questions and more play a role because if you don't start respecting yourself, no one else will. Know your worth and don't allow others to disrespect you. How you present yourself can be the difference in landing your ideal job or relationship. From a professional perspective, you will always represent the organization you work for or if it's your own personal company, people will be reluctant to do business with you. People can usually sense a lack of self-respect by your actions, whether good or bad. Understand that self-respect begins with understanding personal responsibility and upholding your core values you were taught growing up. Stop allowing your emotions to get the best of you. The more you respect you have for yourself, the more you will be able to love yourself.

DEMAND Respect

Respect is Earned, Never Given

For starters, HUMBLE yourself and always keep your word. Always be a problem solver rather than a problem starter. Display your leadership skills by setting clear boundaries and expectations for those around you. Don't ever apologize when you've done nothing wrong, especially when you are speaking the truth about a situation. Avoid behaviors that make you insecure about yourself, because no one will trust you, they will view you as being incompetent and ineffective. In order to gain respect, start developing relationships with others. Whether it's a business relationship or a personal one, a healthy relationship will always carry a high bar for respect. Learn to encourage and protect people around you, stand up for them when it matters most, and they will develop the utmost respect for you.

Chapter Assignment

In this chapter, I viewed Respect as being a wild card in your life simply because it can make or break a deal, or even break your spirit. Growing up, you've heard time and time again, treat others like you would want to be treated. When demanding respect, you must be confident in your abilities. Just talking about greatness is not enough, act on your ambitions. I asked the question, what do you see when you look in the mirror? You should see confidence, pride, and strong-willed individual ready to conquer the day ahead and improve their outlook on life. Your self-respect will translate into respect from others.

BAD INTENTIONS (JOKER)

"Great minds discuss ideas; average minds discuss events; small minds discuss people."
— Eleanor Roosevelt

Belittling Others for Your Benefit

Kill the Gossip

We all know that people love to gossip about things that don't add value to their lives. You see it on the job, church, home, social media, and even in your circle of friends. You find yourself laughing at other people's pain or talking about a bone headed decision they may have made, but in reality, their behavior may be a cry for help. Being mean or teasing someone too much can affect that person's mental stability. Everyone goes through storms that we can't see, so making fun of him or her may not always be a good thing. It may serve as a temporary laugh but you'll be devastated if it led to a person harming themselves. Whenever people begin speaking of negative things around you, kill the gossip. Change the subject, disassociate yourself for the moment, or simply stop carrying the bone. People can pinpoint every wrong about you, but when it comes to correcting themselves the "pen" doesn't work. Prefer to talk about things that everyone can benefit from. Are you going to continue to complain about the gap in disparity or are you going to start doing things to bridge that gap?

Intentional Intimidation

Don't Destroy Your Bridges

The same energy you put out is the same energy you'll get in return. You never know who you'll rub elbows with on a daily basis. People will attempt to wish negative things upon you, but that doesn't necessarily mean you have to accept it. You should never engage in that type of behavior due to the fact you will reap what you sow. You sit back and wonder why things are not moving in your life like they should be, it's because you don't want others around you to be more successful than you are. The crab mentality is real. Instead of allowing someone that's truly capable to enter first, then allow them to open the doors for everyone else to follow suit, you'll fight against the leader so you can accept the recognition. What you're left with is individuals not wanting to neither trust you nor help you when it's needed. You should always be cultivating positive relationships and stay away from those seeking to destroy bridges.

Chapter Assignment

Be great, speak of greatness, act on greatness, and greatness will follow. Having negative intentions will only create failure.

INTELLECT

"Beware of false knowledge, it is more dangerous than ignorance." – *George Bernard Shaw*

Utilize Good Judgment

Be able to Adapt to Change

Intellect is simply common sense, but individuals allow it to lie idle because they get wrapped up in unimportant things and ideas. Intellect is the ability to improve your character and ignore stupidity. Learn from your past experience, take that knowledge and build upon new things that you want to create in your life. Utilize the talents currently you possess to educate your heart and mind, as well as improve your communication skills. You must first be open to new ideas, followed by the willingness to change the way you go about doing things. Start thinking outside the box, because as I mentioned before, how will you expect to live outside the box, with your thought process inside a bubble? Unleash your creative brain and start using the common sense you were born with, you'll be amazed how far it'll take you in life.

Abandon Mediocre Thinking

Be Ambitious with Your Thoughts

Unlock the potential of your mind by allowing your imagination to be limitless. There's nothing wrong with dreaming, but at some point, in life you should want to be ambitious and pursue those dreams. Allow the quality of your thoughts to be great rather than lackluster and uninspiring. An entertainer can provide a mediocre performance and fade away, but someone can have a one hit wonder and possess passion and give an extraordinary performance and that person will be remembered. You may not be that entertainer, but you will impact the lives of those around in some shape or form.

Chapter Assignment

Challenge your intellect daily. It may be reading a book or learning a new skill or even perfecting a hobby. Whatever it may be, focus and inspire your mind to allow yourself to come full circle and become a better you.

PROBLEM SOLVING

"The three great essentials to achieve anything worthwhile are first, hard work; second, stick-to-itiveness; third, common sense."
— Thomas A. Edison

Take a Step Back

Evaluate the Situation

The problems you encounter can possibly result from the root of your actions. You never truly evaluate the cause and effect of a situation because we tend to act on impulse. You're happy when there's a positive outcome, but when the consequences arise, we like to blame others and not take responsibility for the decision. Consider this, did you ask the right questions? Did you find any clarity in the response you received? When it comes to solving problems, you have to cast your net wider within your thought process and seek multiple solutions. Only then will you be able to dissect and define the problem and deliver positive results by your actions.

Develop Your Sense of Discernment

Never Judge Book by its Cover

As you go through life, you'll find that you may need to manage people by their attitudes and personalities. Discernment is the ability to see things for what they really are and not for what you want them to be. Be wise in the way you judge things and people's character. Sometimes you can have a better understanding or even figure out things that others can't. That may be your gift in a way to help others figure out life. During the process, be wise and less judgmental when seeking to solve problems. Once you began to work on your sense of discernment, you'll be able to distinguish the true character of an individual rather than his/her representative.

Chapter Assignment

Knowing how to manage people and problems well is one of the most important skills in life you can have. Build upon that foundation by understanding the bones of any situation, so when you start to create solutions to a problem you'll have a better understanding. Sometimes the first solution is not always the best one, so take into consideration additional feedback.

BAD ATTITUDE

"You must be the change you wish to see in the world."
– Gandhi

Challenging Circumstances

Choose Love and Joy

You can't always control the circumstances that occur in life, but it's how you respond to the situation that will determine your attitude. As individuals living in a fast-paced society, we have developed a sense of wanting things right away. Yet when things don't go as planned, you already know what happens next, you develop a bad attitude. Have you ever considered the idea of not taking life so seriously? How about forgiving the limitations of others. Everyone doesn't share your same vision nor will they be able to do things at the pace or level that you can, so rather than develop a bad attitude, give others a chance. Always show your gratitude towards others, a simple thank you will go a long way. Finally, use your setbacks to improve your attitude. If you happen to experience a sense of rejection, reflect back on your previous actions and determine how you can improve going forward.

Get in Front of Conflict

Resolve Issues Early

Your attitude will certainly define who you are. Having a bad attitude is a challenge that's difficult to overcome. You can tell yourself that you won't act a certain way, but then a person will say or do something and we're right back in that state of mind with a bad attitude. Developing a bad attitude will bring about immaturity, it will put your heart in a negative place, damage relationships, and even convert you into a selfish mode. So how do we resolve issues that put us in that state of mind? There's numerous ways, but you have to find what works best for you. My three suggestions involve praying, removing self from situation, and showing resolve. My mother always told me to pray for yourself and others, especially those who you're upset with or may have done something to you. Always attempt to remove yourself from the situation to prevent yourself from allowing ignorance to get the best of you. Either walk away, attempt to change the subject, or simply kill them with kindness and a smile. Finally, use resolve and always approach negativity with an open heart and mind, because sometimes what you say can cut a person deep, and although that wound may heal, it will certainly leave scars. You know yourself better than anyone else, so seek the best methods to help you cope.

Chapter Assignment

Adjust your attitude daily and rid yourself of toxic people and thoughts. Stop holding everyone else accountable for his or her negative attitude, but then attempt to justify your own poor attitude. Continue to pray, remove, and resolve.

OPPORTUNITIES

"Success is not final, failure is not fatal: it is the
courage to continue what counts."
- Winston Churchill

Don't be Afraid of Opportunity

When Doors Open, Enter

In order to succeed, you have to be great at seizing opportunity whenever it presents itself. Opportunity inspires us to take chances on things that will make your life better. Opportunity usually comes unexpectedly during times when you are distracted or too busy drawing opinions of this can't be true. Opportunity often looks like hard work and if you're not willing to roll those sleeves up, it'll be a missed one. How many times have you been asked to do things or go places and your response was no, only later to find out that was the opportunity you were looking for? Trust your intuition and start taking chances; it will take you along the right path fit for you. Taking on opportunity can be frightening, especially considering the unknown. You're going to fall down, but if so, learn to fall forward. Keep in mind that just because one door closes, there are always other windows of opportunity that will open in the process. The experience of following through might just be what changes your life forever.

Mistaken Identity

Don't Miss Out

You may feel unlucky at times wondering why certain people are extremely lucky and consistently winning but you never do. Luck often times is a result of individuals being in the right place at the right time. They put themselves in that position with positive thoughts that they expect to win. Successful individuals don't rely on luck, when they experience missed opportunity, they put themselves in a position to where they won't miss the next one. Do you want to continue living a life of "oh wells" or one of "what ifs?" If opportunity comes knocking at your door, answer it with the intention of saying yes. If you are persistent and want success, you keep knocking at the door and eventually it will open.

Chapter Assignment

Challenge yourself this month that you are going to create new opportunities for yourself. All problems are usually an opportunity in disguise. Stop hesitating because opportunities can be short-lived, but they are also all around us at any given time. Meet new people because most times it's not what you know but whom you know.

DEPRESSION

*"You will face many defeats in life, but never let
yourself be defeated."*   *— Maya Angelou*

Emotional State of Mind

Origins of Depression

Majority of the time, unknowingly, depression can
often result from things that occurred during
childhood. Maybe your childhood wasn't the greatest
and you found yourself being compared to other kids.
Fast forward to present day and you still find yourself
making the same comparisons with older peers.
Depression can often be self-imposed based on things
you are searching for, such as love, happiness, etc.
Ever find yourself arranging for something you badly
want only to have it not happened? You find that you
are more irritable, frustrated, argumentative, and can't
seem to make your mind up. On a personal note, I've
found myself having one drink at night only to turn
into several drinks, then trying to convince myself that
I had a long day at work. I can distinctly remember my

mother saying, "don't try to drink your problems away". I had come to the realization that I was somewhat depressed along with other signs. I had reached low points in life and found myself settling and becoming complacent. The results due to lack of consistency can often lead to you not feeling worthy. It would be safe to say that most of us are simply a facade of what we should be on the outside, but on the inside feeling broken and out of touch with reality.

Develop Coping Mechanisms

Improving Your Mood

One particular way you can begin to start improving your mood is changing the way you think. Something as simple as your thoughts can have a major impact on your outcome on life. Seeking outlets such as changing your diet, outdoor activities, and physical fitness to focus on your total well-being. Also, stop neglecting your physical well-being and appearance, because not caring how you look on the outside is a strong indicator of problems happening on the inside. Try writing in a journal and put on paper of what you feel on the inside, because harboring those emotions will only make you slide deeper into a depressive state. Finally, seek professional help and talk to someone who is unbiased and can help you express yourself in a way that you will begin to start feeling happy again.

Chapter Assignment

To combat depression, think back on the joyous moments in your life. I'm sure your good days far outweigh your bad ones. List your accomplishments if you have to and reflect on them. Stop allowing negative thoughts to be intrusive of your positive mindset. Create that expectation for yourself because no one else will. Simply take control of your thoughts and actions. Finally, you should laugh more and often, and most importantly pray.

REGRET

> *"Sometimes you to take a step back to move forward."*
> *– Erika Taylor*

Move on from Your Past

Rid Yourself of Self-Pity

Regrets are about bad choices of something you did or failed to do. We've all dealt with regret at some point in our lives and I'm pretty sure if asked, you could name a few opportunities, and possibly a laundry list of things. You probably replayed scenarios over and over of things that make all the difference in the world, and you found you developed the *could-a, would-a, should-a* blues. Ponder this, are you angry with yourself for having had the correct information to make a decision, but made the wrong one instead? Do you wish you had spoken up for someone in harm's way and didn't, not reaching your full potential in life, or the most common reason, you failed to communicate with someone hat one last time not realizing that they would pass away? It's happened to me several occasions and boy was I ever regretful and vowed not to allow it to happen again. Time is precious so make sure you make every minute count. You can't rewind the past, but you can most certainly forgive yourself and move forward.

Make Every Moment Count

Seek and Learn from Lessons

Regret keeps you stuck in the past, so you have to ask yourself an important question, what do I need to do in order to move forward? Keep in mind that we all make mistakes, so the first step would be to forgive yourself of past actions. Understand that you truly did the best that you could at that time. Until you accept that notion, you will continue to experience regret. Follow your dreams rather than other people's opinion because you have the ability to right your ship and prove others wrong. How many times growing up or even in your adult years you heard the phrase, "you'll never amount to anything?" Hearing that statement should have motivated you to not only prove them wrong, but to show yourself what you are truly capable of. One of your biggest regrets should always be that of not trying. Take in this perspective, when you're constantly looking behind you, you fail to notice what's right in front of you.

Chapter Assignment

Remind yourself that you are only human. Learn more about yourself and view your past as a lesson learned. Start holding yourself accountable for decisions made. Finally, be proactive rather than reactive with your responses to your past.

DREAM BIG (JOKER)

"Our greatest fear should not be of failure... but of succeeding at things in life that don't really matter."
— Francis Chan

Reach for the Stars

Make Your Dreams Reality

Dreams are an important part of who you are. Dreams are often a source of your inner wisdom. Every success story ever documented all the way down to your own personal successes all began with a dream. It's up to you to realize that you can create and accomplish anything you put your mind too. The problem by not reaching full potential and living out those dreams are reasons of fear and discouragement from others. You have the ability to determine how big you want the dream to be and how soon you're going to make it your reality. Step out on Faith, trust God, and you'll begin to see and experience the things you've always imagined.

The Future Belongs to You

Develop the Courage to Pursue

You can create anything you put your mind too so please allow your imagination to flow freely. Don't place any limitations on your expectations because you don't want to stand in your own way of success. We can be our own worst critics at times, so believe strongly in your abilities to get things done. Throughout my teaching career, from day one I set the tone by thanking my students for developing the courage to pursue a new career. Especially those who were able to raise a family, go to work, yet still manage to make it to class. I've even taught a couple students who were homeless, but wanted to change their circumstances so bad, that they went onto become successful. Although this chapter is about dreaming big, you still need to become a doer and put those ideas into motion. Reinforce your progress by reflecting on your milestones to keep you motivated about your progress. Lastly, be fearless in your approach of your dreams.

Chapter Insight

Three Life Rules

1. *If you don't go after what you want, you'll never have it.*
2. *If you don't ask, the answer will always be no.*
3. *If you don't step forward, you'll always be in the same place.*
   - Unknown

Chapter Assignment

Dreams don't work unless you do. Continue to pursue your dreams and don't allow individuals to discourage your efforts. The look on the face of your doubters will be priceless and self-gratifying once you achieve those goals.

Recreate Yourself

"It had long since come to my attention that people of accomplishment rarely sat back and let things happen to them. They went out and happened to things."
— Leonardo Da Vinci

Create Your New Reality

Get Your House in Order

The phrase, "get your house in order" is not meant as a euphemism; you must literally get your house in order. Priorities, emotions, and relationships, need to have structure in your life in order for you to progress. Ever wonder why things don't go as planned or usually results in a negative outcome? As people, when spend our lives settling for less and not pursuing what truly makes us happy. You have a tendency to be concerned about the other person feelings, yet hold we hold onto feelings of regret, anger, resentment, and frustrations and bury them on the inside. You're afraid of starting over, always wondering how others will view you, and you don't want to disappoint others' expectations because they may view your situation as "ideal." You feel like you can't become the person you want to be because you feel obligated. The only person you should be concerned with is yourself and once you're in a better place, you can be a more effective friend, better spouse, and family member. Changing yourself takes time, trial and error, and most importantly patience on your behalf. Start making a conscious effort to improve and be honest with your pursuit of creating a new reality.

Brand Your Image

Fire Your Representative

Get rid of the person you were and start becoming the person you want to be. People always change, sometimes good or bad, but as individuals you should always seek new ways of self-improvement. In Chapter 5, I asked you to complete a SWOT analysis of your personal life. Considering the results, it isn't just about knowing your strengths and weaknesses, but also opening yourself up to new opportunities, develop a new way of thinking, ability to try new things, and building new relationships. It can be a difficult task when you continue to trust your old way of thinking when all it's ever done was let you down and/or kept you from reaching your goals. Be willing to adjust your self-image based on what's going on in your life right now as opposed to a past version of yourself. You may have had poor communication skills years ago, but now you've found communication to be more effective now because you listen more. You probably used to be good at a lot of things that you're no longer good at, but that's the old you and the new person you see in the mirror is waiting to flourish. Look at the diagram below and identify traits that describe you and those you can improve upon.

Chapter Assignment

Choose right now rather than tomorrow to start becoming the best person you can possibly be. Your life was once affected by the decisions you've made in the past, but your future will be determined by the choices you make today. You can be amazed with opportunities simply by changing your habits and thinking positively. Everything you're in search of in life begins and ends with your decision-making process. Continue to be ambitious in your pursuit of success and happiness; it's your destiny.

Conclusion

In closing, I hope this book serves as a helpful guide for you to start winning at this game called LIFE. It has been my pleasure to share my ideas and personal examples with each of you in an attempt to encourage you to seek greatness. You're not alone when enduring hardships, but it's how we overcome adversity, which builds your character. I leave you with my final thought, ***"SOMETIMES WE CAN'T CONTROL THE CARDS THAT WE ARE DEALT IN LIFE, BUT WE CAN DETERMINE THE OUTCOME."***

- Kwantrell D. Green

ABOUT THE AUTHOR

Kwantrell D. Green is an entrepreneur, business coach, and motivational speaker here to show you how to WIN at this game called Life. As we all know, life can be very challenging and throw all types of curve balls. He consistently coaches individuals to understand that with every obstacle faced, opportunities are created. Raised by a single mom and grandparents that constantly supported yet disciplined his actions, molded him into the successful entrepreneur he is today.

Graduate of University of Southern Mississippi and William Carey University. Kwantrell is very passionate about helping elderly people and children, but also developed a niche for educating and motivating young adults, which has led to a 14-year career in teaching at career colleges. With a strong personal attitude and belief of "Aspire to be Great, that's what God wants you to be," in 2007 he opened his first successful business providing adult day care and home health services. Considering his passion for helping people develop personally and professionally, he decided to focus on community advocacy and human development.

From there, the LIFE POKER Series was born. He currently serves on a community health center's board and spends time empowering/mentoring our youth to be future community leaders of tomorrow. He currently operates a consulting business in healthcare marketing, participates in speaking engagements, and exercises his passion for teaching and growing others.

A family man at heart, he's a loving husband and father of three beautiful daughters. Also a member of Omega Psi Phi Fraternity, Inc., which he exemplifies what it means to be an Omega Man. He enjoys giving back, serving the community, and has a strong affinity for helping seniors and kids, but also understands the importance of reaching everyone.

Always keep in mind, "Sometimes we can't control the cards that are dealt in life, but we can determine the outcome." – Kwantrell Green

60838496R00089

Made in the USA
Columbia, SC
18 June 2019